THE EXTREMELY SERIOUS GUIDE TO CLASS

THE EXTREMELY SERIOUS GUIDE TO CLASS

KEITH RAY

COLUMBUS BOOKS
LONDON

Other books in the *Extremely Serious* series:
The Extremely Serious Guide to Fitness and Health
The Extremely Serious Guide to Sex
The Extremely Serious Guide to Business
The Extremely Serious Guide to Parenthood
The Extremely Serious Guide to Moving House
The Extremely Serious Guide to Sin
The Extremely Serious Guide to Gardening

First published in Great Britain in 1988 by
Columbus Books Limited
19-23 Ludgate Hill, London EC4M 7PD

Designed by Rupert Kirby, London

Typeset by Falcon Graphic Art Ltd
Wallington, Surrey
Printed and bound by Adlard & Son Limited,
Letchworth, Herts

ISBN 0 86287 435 1

CONTENTS

'Just look at the state of you – no tie, torn shirt . . . What sort of class do you want people to think we're from?'

BEFORE YOU READ THIS BOOK . . .

- Have you ever wondered exactly what class is?
- Do you imagine being upper-class must be real fun, or do you think it is just like being from any other class once the novelty has worn off?
- Has *your* novelty ever worn off, and are you aware how very painful it can be?
- Do you ever wonder why some people pronounce 'class' to rhyme with 'arse' whilst others pronounce 'class' to rhyme with 'ass'? And did you know there's a man living in Hemel Hempstead who pronounces 'class' to rhyme with 'bovine spongiform encephalitis'?
- Do you think it's more upper-class to say 'arse' than 'bottom'? And what about people who call it 'bum', 'backside', 'derrière', 'rump', 'posterior', 'bottie', 'sit-upon', 'nether regions' or 'Chancellor of the Exchequer'?
- Do the upper classes have bums at all? Do dukes and earls, and even the Pope, actually go to the toilet and wipe their bottoms? Or do they have servants (or cardinals) to go to the toilet on their behalf?
- What about sex? Do the upper classes exclaim at the moment of orgasm, 'Oh, that's jolly spiffing! What a super wheeze!'
- Do the upper classes ever have orgasms out of season?
- Are aristocratic erections, like aristocratic homes, more stately than commoners' ones, and are they ever subject to preservation orders?
- If you had an erection which had a preservation order stamped on it how would *you* keep it up, or would the mere act of stamping be sufficient?
- Does class really matter in the global context of nuclear disarmament, balance of payment problems, world peace and leaving the top off the toothpaste tube?
- Can you tell a person's class from his appearance?
- Can you tell a parson's class from his appearance?
- Is there an 'upper-class' smell?
- Can you change your class, and if so is it easy like changing your socks or difficult like changing your sex? Does class, like socks and sex, get dirty – and if so, what do you do about it?
- Can you change your class, socks and sex all at the same time, without waking your partner up? And when he or she wakes up which change do you think will be noticed first?

- Is it significant that 'class' is nearly, but not quite, an anagram of 'lasso', a word that originated in Spain, a country that borders France, the very country where the Cluniac order of friars separated from the Benedictines in the eleventh century, the very century during which the Vikings were beaten at the Battle of Clontarf by the Irish under the leadership of Brian Boru, the very man who, had he been born 916 years later and been called John Logie Baird, might well have invented the television and hence been responsible for the screening of such programmes as *Till Death Us Do Part*, a series with a title containing five words, five being – amazingly – the very same number of letters as there are in the word 'class'? Or is it just a coincidence?

If questions such as these really fascinate you then you are a right nerd. But don't let that stop you reading the book.

'I wuz born wiv a silver spoon in me mouth. It wuz the only place me old Dad could fink of 'iding the loot!'

WHY THIS BOOK EXISTS

Class is very important. It's one of those things, like age and sex, that belongs to all of us (Ed.: *Speak for yourself, duckie . . . I've got plenty of age but the sex has been in short supply recently*). And although we may not like it, just as we may not like our age or our sex (Ed.: *Now you're talking! I like* my *sex, it's the other sex that leaves me cold*), it is very difficult, if not impossible, to alter our class once we have been born into it. Mind you, it is very difficult to define class, or say why one person is upper-class whilst another is lower-class, or indeed what class we belong to ourselves. In many ways class is in the eye of the beholder. It is a bit like bad breath – difficult to tell if you have it yourself, but everyone else knows.

When I first bounced the idea of writing a book on class off my family and friends it got a pretty cold reception. 'I forecast it will be marginally suboptimal from a marketing economics point of view,' my wife declared . . . well, in fact, her precise words were 'You must be stark raving bonkers. Who's going to buy that? And when are you going to finish putting up those cupboards in the kitchen?'

My son was equally supportive. 'Oh, not *another* book, Daddy. When are you going to help me repair my radio-controlled car?' Actually those weren't *his* precise words either; his *precise* words resulted in a week's TV ban and loss of pocket money.

Luckily things picked up a bit when I suggested the idea to my agent and publisher. I can't remember the exact conversation, but it went something like this:

AGENT	Right, what do you intend to put in this class book that'll make it more exciting than a knee in the groin in a grotty Salford suburb on a wet afternoon in March? [*Actually, that sounded quite exciting to me.*]
ME	Well, I thought I'd talk about class, and taste, and things like garden gnomes . . .
PUBLISHER	. . . and how they reflect a repressed auto-regressive middle-class tendency towards rampant gnomophilia? Yes, yes, and what else . . .?
ME	Well, maybe a bit on the historical context of present-day upper-class confidence . . .
AGENT	. . . and things like *droit de seigneur*, and how lust-crazed belted earls ravish young virgins in the stable, pressing their silky, throbbing thighs hard into the rough straw . . . yes, yes, go on, I'm beginning to like it . . .

ME	. . . and then maybe a page or two on how to ascertain your own class . . .
PUBLISHER	. . . perhaps in terms of how many strokes with a suede-covered trade union membership card are required to provoke an uncontrollable erection during the TUC conference dinner? Great, and . . .
ME	. . . obviously a bit on the class tendencies of famous people from the past . . .
AGENT	. . . like Hannibal, whose uncontrollable urge to be alone with young, nymphomaniac war-elephants was a reflection of his upbringing in a typical upper-middle-class Carthaginian household where his unnatural feelings towards the family dog had their first manifestations. . .
PUBLISHER	. . . and then we could lead naturally into the Romans, perhaps with a double-page spread on Caligula, orgies, necrophilia, rampant bestiality . . .
AGENT	. . . showing how the working-class slaves were brutally exploited by the sex-crazed patrician class and forced to participate in practices which couldn't even be referred to in writing in Caligula's time.
PUBLISHER	We'll also need a few spicy bits of course: not enough to detract from the core subject of class – just an odd smattering or two . . .
AGENT	. . . like how you reveal your true class at the moment of orgasm . . .
PUBLISHER	. . . and what to say the morning after you've spent an explosive night with the two under-age daughters of a premier duke, only to find they were really his two elder sons who have had sex-change ops . . .
AGENT	. . . and whether the curtsey symbolizes offering oral sex to the sovereign . . .
PUBLISHER	. . . and whether the use of a sword in conferring knighthoods has phallic connotations . . .
AGENT	. . . and whether it's significant that the word 'class', when said with a mouth full of peanuts, sounds remarkably like the Swahili word for premature ejaculation . . .
PUBLISHER	. . . or whatever seems appropriate . . .

As I said, I can't remember the conversation in too much detail because at this point I left the room and caught the bus home. It was a good six hours before the other two even noticed, and several months before the grins faded from their faces. However, there was an indication that class might be an acceptable subject provided certain criteria were satisfied. So I bashed out a quick draft. A few elephants (Hannibal for the use of), orgies (inspired by Emperor Caligula), phallic connotations and nymphomaniac fantasies later, the book acquired its present form.

THE ORIGINS OF CLASS AS WE KNOW IT TODAY

In the beginning, class did not exist. The Garden of Eden proclaimed no desirable semi-detacheds, Filofaxes, Golf GTi's, green wellies, country clubs, private schools or medical insurance, and Adam and Eve came from a similar social background . . . if you can call a rib a social background.

However, upon expulsion from the Garden of Eden, Adam and Eve quickly discovered that some parts of God's great firmament were more desirable than others. The estate agents of the time would no doubt have said, if there had been any (I know – it's difficult to imagine a time when there weren't estate agents, and certainly Eden High Street must have been a pretty bleak place): 'Desirable ¼ acre of firmament within level walking distance of Eden's gates', 'Much-sought-after area within apple-throwing distance of Tree of Knowledge', 'Much improved property ideally suited to serpent owners' and so on. Thus some of Adam and Eve's offspring came to live in better areas than others, and as a result started to feel superior. This is where the division between the upper and the lower class started.

Back in those times you were born either upper- or lower-class, and you remained in your respective social slot until you died. As the two classes lived alongside each other, and experienced much the same sort of activities and events, they developed quite similar outlooks on life. (Even today the highest and lowest classes share many views in common.) This situation lasted for thousands of years, until one day God decided that man was ready for the net curtain; 'net', with its gossamer-like connotations, might seem to be a bit of a misnomer in view of the curtains' first incarnation as strips of festering cow-hide and rotting sheep's entrails bonded together with a mixture of pig's dung and chicken's blood . . . but the basic effect was the same, even if the smell was different. From the day a member of the lower class first decided to hang one of these prototype net curtains over the door of his cave, he instantly felt superior to his neighbours (at whom he could peer from behind the curtain, provided he held his nose). However, he hadn't *become* upper-class. He couldn't, because he wasn't born into the upper class. So he had to become something halfway in between, and so started the in-between class.

The new three-class system of upper, in-between and lower lasted a further few thousand years until society started to get more complex. People began to mass-produce net curtains, and an entrepreneurial class came into being. Special caves were opened where the curtains were sold, and thus a shop-keeper class emerged; others started developing finer combinations of cow-hide and entrails, and sought odour-free adhesives to replace the pig's dung and chicken blood, and thus a scientist class emerged, and so on. This resulted in far greater class mobility. Also by this time the appellation 'in-between' for the class that was neither upper nor lower had been dropped, because some misguided Stone Age peasant thought it sounded similar to the word meaning 'unbridled incestuous sexual intercourse between illiterate, unwashed, transvestite night-soil collectors' (in fact he was mistaken, and merely wished to gain cheap publicity) and the modern term 'middle class' had come into use.

However, the increased social mobility had a profound and lasting effect. The people descending into the middle class from the upper class thought themselves vastly superior to those rising to the middle class from the lower class; as a result the idea of upper-middle and lower-middle emerged around the core of the existing middle (or, as it now became known, the middle-middle) class. As time passed the structure became even more complex. People who moved to the middle-middle class from above as a result of reduced personal circumstances still saw themselves as a cut above their neighbours who had risen above their lower-middle origins, and so in turn there emerged an upper-middle-middle class and a lower-middle-middle class. Thus the process has continued ever since, until nowadays we have about 14 million quite distinct social levels, amongst which I believe I myself am upper-middle-middle-lower-upper-lower-middle-middle-lower-middle-middle class.

For the purpose of this book, however, I have adopted the simplified system of classes known technically as the 'Pet Dog' or Rover system, which is roughly as follows:

Upper class	These are the people who wouldn't be seen dead in a Rover because some of their servants drive second-hand ones.
Upper-middle class	These are the people who can remember the time when all they could afford was a Rover, but who now can afford 'better' things.
Middle-middle class	These are the core of people who actually drive around (whilst the cars remain functional, that is) in Rovers.
Lower-middle class	These are the people who aspire to owning a Rover.
Working class	These are the people who actually *make* the Rovers, and because of the way they make them wouldn't be seen dead in one, even if given it for free!

AN ALTERNATIVE DEFINITION OF THE CLASS SYSTEM

HEALTH WARNING
This is a full-strength definition of the class system, not to be used by those of a weak disposition

For a start you can forget all that pompous crap about socio-economic groups, population census classifications and all that load of vomit. You see, your actual class system is a sort of sociological continuum, if you get my drift. At one extreme you've got your toffee-nosed chinless gits, your Henry-stocracy, with their hunt balls, titles, pedigrees, debs and about as much brain as you could balance on the end of a bi-sexual mosquito's willie, whilst at the other extreme you've got your real plebs, the fermenting dungheap of society, who possess about as much natural culture and refinement as a 4-day-old spent incontinence pad, and who are about as welcome in the world of the nobs as a fart in a lift. In between these sociological poles all of the rest of us, the diarrhoea of society, exist in one continuous smear from semi-pleb to semi-nob, a nauseating morass of sycophantic, self-conscious, net-curtained and privet-hedged pigswill. So basically we're all either Henries, dungheaps or pigswill.

'If it's any consolation, only pedigree *dogs get it.'*

DO YOU NEED TO READ THIS BOOK?

'It's not that I'm questioning what's on your c.v. . . . I'm just wondering what made the son of a duke do a PhD in embroidery.'

This book is all about class and what it means. (This should come as no great surprise to the reader, in view of the book's title. Any reader who bought it and got this far under the misconception that it is about the treatment of fungal foot infections amongst pregnant South American vampire bats should therefore accept that he or she is not numbered among the intellectual giants of this planet. But then, the world would be a very boring place if everyone were an intellectual giant.) The key question is, having bought it, do you actually need to read it, or should you do one of the other exciting things with it listed in the next section: 'Exciting Things To Do With This Book Other Than Read It.' To decide whether or not you need to read the book answer the following questions and add up how many 'yes' answers you gave. Then assess whether you need to continue reading by referring to the notes at the end.

Do you wish to find out:

- whether colonic irrigation is an acceptable topic of conversation at a Buckingham Palace Garden Party?
- the etiquette for passing the port at the Lord Mayor's Banquet when you discover the diner next to you has no arms?
- whether it is in fact better to wait until you go to the loo before passing the port, particularly if you are in the throes of granting arms to the diner next to you?
- the correct form of apology to use when you have accidentally splashed the trousers of the Lord Privy Seal in the gents' urinals at the House of Lords?
- the correct form of letter to write to a reigning monarch when you have farted whilst being introduced to him or her, and whether it should be written on lined paper or not?
- the correct form of address for a duke's illegitimate daughter's husband's gay lover's transsexual uncle's mistress who was formerly the second bigamous wife of a premier bishop's widowed sister's stepfather-in-law?
- whether the working class derives more pleasure from removing ear wax and trimming nostril hairs than the aristocracy?
- the correct shape of glass for serving Babycham to members of the royal family?
- the only foolproof way of establishing whether the yuppie sitting next to you on the Underground actually has an erection or merely carries his Filofax in an unusual place?
- an appropriately inoffensive exclamation to make when you discover that the delightful nymphomaniac you have just undressed in your hotel room is actually the transvestite Bishop of Rochdale?

If you answered 'yes' to all ten questions then you certainly need to read on. If you answered 'yes' to at least none of them, then reading on is strongly recommended. If you had to lie through your teeth in order to answer 'yes' to even none of them, then you should still read on. If you had to borrow someone else's teeth to lie through, and this brought on a spontaneous erection owing to a false teeth fetish, then wait until the excitement dies down before reading on (and return the teeth first). If returning the teeth brought on a second erection owing to a weird false-teeth-returning fetish, and you are actually female, please write to the author c/o the publisher.

'I never promised that private health care would be perfect.'

'Look, if you've got four working-class exploiting capitalists, and you take away two working-class exploiting capitalists, how many working-class exploiting capitalists have you got left?'

EXCITING THINGS TO DO WITH THIS BOOK OTHER THAN READ IT

If it is inappropriate for you to read this book (for example, if you can't read, or you haven't got the time, or you haven't got the inclination, or you are so fat you can't get the book close enough to make out the print, or you are too busy copulating to break off for a read, etc.) then there are many other useful things that can be done with it to salvage something of its cover price. Listed below are some suggestions.

- Turn it into a nourishing soup: take ½ pint chicken stock, 2 carrots, a small onion (chopped), a clove of garlic, ¼ lb diced smoked ham and a bouquet garni. Boil all the ingredients together for about 45 minutes. Add salt and pepper to taste, and this book. Just before serving remove the bouquet garni and the book. This makes a delicious and amusingly different soup.

- Convert it into an unusual and conversation-provoking condom. Tear the book up into small pieces and add to ½ pint cold water. Bring to the boil and simmer for 1 hour until a smooth *papier mâché* is formed. Stir in 3 dessertspoons wallpaper paste, and leave to cool. When cool apply to the erect male organ until a solid layer 1 inch (2.5 cm) thick is formed. Allow the mixture to harden. The condom is now ready for use. It may also be painted using a suitable non-toxic paint, and if it is treated with a coat of clear varnish it may be re-used after washing. This makes a most economical form of contraception.

- Make an interesting table decoration out of it. Soak the book in a suitable high-quality wall tile adhesive, and whilst still wet press intriguing objects into it (such as spent condoms, live sparrows, dirty underwear, Access receipts for massage parlour services, and unusual amputated limbs, obtained from a reputable source). Allow to harden, and then use as the centrepiece on the table at intellectual dinner parties. Watch your guests gasp with amazement at your skill, and listen to the stimulating discussion about the decline of true rural crafts that is sure to follow.

- Turn it into a useful domestic appliance by drilling a neat hole in one corner and threading a strong 2-foot-long leather thong through it. If you now whirl it round your head you will find it has many uses ranging from keeping the children in order to castrating stray cats. It may also be used as a cheap form of remote control for the TV.

- Recycle it as a set of boxer shorts. Carefully separate the individual pages and sellotape them together into the pattern of a pair of boxer shorts: a very economical answer to the underwear problem (take care not to dress or undress too quickly however as the paper tends to be rather sharp).

- Transform it into an economical family pet. For this you will need a good-quality adhesive, a very sharp pair of scissors, a felt-tip pen, a bucket of water and a cat. Carefully drown the cat, and then remove all its fur with the scissors. Glue the fur all over the book leaving just one small area blank. In this blank area draw a pleasant face with the felt-tip pen. This creates a much cheaper-to-run, cleaner and quieter pet than the cat ever was, and if the cat's pleasant warmth is missed the book may be gently heated up in a moderate oven for about 10-15 minutes, taking care not to singe the fur. There is no need to have the book neutered or to stock up with anti-flea powder.

- If none of the foregoing ideas appeals, the book may be turned into a tasteful imitation Bible by glueing some maroon leathercloth over the outside and burning the shape of a cross on to the front cover with a hot soldering iron. If no maroon leathercloth is available try green Dralon or, as a last resort, cat skin (for what to do with the rest of the cat send off for a booklet of tasty recipes, obtainable direct from the author c/o the St Joseph's Mission for Hopelessly Sick Authors, Gut House, Offal Street, Catford).

'First thing tomorrow I'm going to write to Eton and demand a refund.'

'. . . *I thought I recognized the old school chains!*'

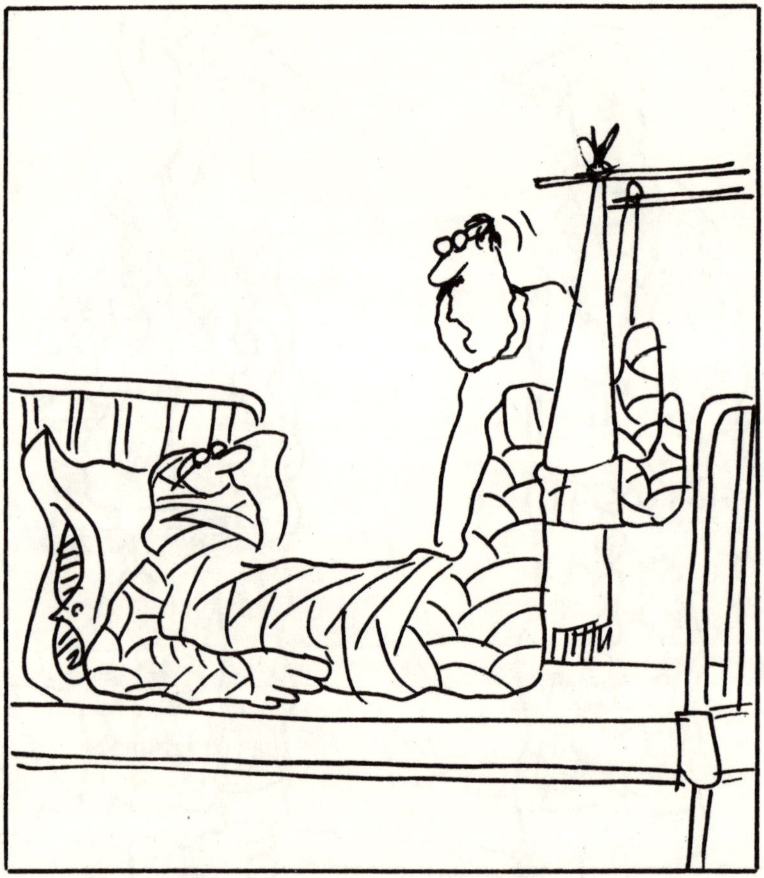

'If it's any consolation, it was a Rolls-Royce that knocked you down.'

THE THINGS PEOPLE SAY ABOUT CLASS

The things people say about class, and particularly about other people's class, reveal a lot about their true character and background. Some examples of what people say, as opposed to what they really mean, are given below:

'They're so common.'	They belong to the class we'd prefer to forget we belong to as well.
'They're not our class.'	They don't belong to the class we'd like to pretend we belong to.
'They're *so* middle-class.'	They're just like us.
'They're *terribly* middle-class.'	They're *exactly* like us, but there's no way we're going to admit it.
'People of *our* class don't do that.'	People of the class we'd like to belong to don't do that, although to be honest we're only guessing because we don't really know anybody of that class.
'I can't abide people like *that*.'	. . . that is, people like us manifesting the sort of behaviour we'd prefer to forget we indulge in.
'They're so stuck up.'	They're higher-class than we are, and that's really annoying.
'They're *such* snobs.'	Like us, they pretend to belong to a higher class than they really are, but somehow *they* get away with it.
'We're not snobs.'	Of course we're snobs, otherwise we wouldn't even think of mentioning it.
'It doesn't matter to us what class anyone is.'	It doesn't matter so long as they're at least from as high a class as us.
'We take everyone at face value regardless of class.'	We only mix with our own class, so that's a fairly safe thing to do.
'I don't mind what class of boy Caroline goes out with . . .'	. . . but I'll *kill* her if she dares to marry beneath her.
'I can't abide class prejudice.'	Someone has just mistaken us for members of a lower class than the one to which we belong.
'Of course, this is a very high-class neighbourhood.'	. . . but if we didn't tell you you'd never realize because it looks exactly like everywhere else.
'They're such a nice, pleasant couple, really.'	They're from a lower social stratum than us.
'Class is not important to us.'	Thank God we're now of a high enough class not to have to worry any more.

'How can anyone accuse this club of being class-prejudiced? Why, anyone who can afford the entry fee of £15,000 is free to join!'

UPPER-CLASS CONSERVATISM

The enduring feature of the upper class is a fundamental conservatism – not of the political sort, but rather a trait of character reflecting a natural moderation, caution and aversion to change. After all, if you live in a stately home that has taken, say, 400 years to achieve its current state of refined dilapidation, and if you can trace your ancestry back to William the Conqueror, it is understandable that you should prefer things to stay much as they are. This inherent conservatism is perhaps best observed in the way the upper class dresses. To the upper class clothes are like an old friend, not to be abandoned at the whim of fashion, but to be preserved and nurtured over the years. After all, why waste money buying fashionable clothes if your old ones still have a quarter of a century of good life left in them?

Let's look at some of the key components of the upper-class gentleman's wardrobe:

Shoes To the upper class there is only one sort of shoe to consider, the all-leather, welted, hand-lasted, heavy brogue made by one of the longer-established companies of gentlemen's shoemakers. They *must* be lace-ups; slip-ons are worn only by men of dubious character, seducers, con-men and people engaged in trade, while synthetic soles are the preserve of the pimp and such-like. Upper-class shoes are not really worn in until they are about eight years old and have been re-heeled three times and re-soled twice. They may then, with luck, stay in their prime for a further 17 years, after which they will decline gracefully into old age. Their decline becomes more serious after 20 years, at which time they may be retired into a more leisurely lifestyle as garden shoes, in which capacity they should function quite happily into their forties or fifties. Before their eighth birthday a new pair of such brogues are like strangers, to be talked to but treated with some degree of caution lest they become excessively familiar. Within the 40- or 50-year life of a decent pair of shoes there is clearly no room for talk of fashion.It is said that one well-known earl held more lavish birthday parties for his favourite pair of shoes than he ever did for his wife; after all, he reasoned, his wife might well leave him after only 20 or 30 years of marriage, but a decent pair of brogues lasts a lifetime.

Jackets Rather like a fine wine or a good Stilton, jackets mature with age. And just as you wouldn't send a cheese to the dry cleaners or wash a fine claret, so you should let a jacket ripen naturally until the full flavour matures. Apart from being worn frequently, a good jacket should be left alone to acquire the dignity that comes only with age. Over its first ten years of life the good tweed jacket from, say, Gieves & Hawkes should acquire that exquisite patina of wet labrador, spilled port, pipe tobacco, fresh-caught salmon and saddle soap that epitomizes the aroma of the English upper class. Below the age of ten a jacket, like a child, can't be relied on to behave itself in public, and might occasionally emit an embarrassing whiff of newness. The best jackets are between 15 and 20 years old.

Suits Unless there is a wedding, funeral or formal social event to attend, suits are simply not worn. Suits suggest you have to work for a living, and no self-respecting upper-class person does that if he can help it. Far better to be seen in jeans.

Trousers Only cavalry twill, or, for the young fogey, corduroy, can complement the dignity of the heavy tweed jacket. The quality of the trousers should be at least on a par with that of the jacket so that they share a similar life expectancy, although even in the most staunchly upper-class household it is accepted that cavalry twills might just require a spot of dry-cleaning every ten or 15 years.

Hats Basically only one sort of hat will do, the felt tweed cap. Deerstalkers are now the affectation of the aspiring upper-middle,whilst bowlers, trilbies and so on are strictly for the plebeian. The golden rule is that the cap *must not* match the jacket, for that would smack of the vulgar whim of fashion.

Shirts White shirts are totally out: they stink of offices, work and the middle class. The only safe shirt is the thick, pure cotton, discreet check model with the slightly floppy collar. After a good five years of wearing in, being washed regularly every two weeks whether dirty or not, the shirt should stand as a fitting companion to the upper-class tweed and twill.

The true gentleman's wardrobe is notable for its economy. Although the initial purchase price may be high, each item's life expectancy (between 20 and 30 years) makes the running cost quite modest – indeed, only a fraction of that of the trendy middle class who buy 'fashion' clothes on impulse and replace their wardrobe even before it has gained its majority. (It is interesting to note that although all the above comments were intended to apply to gentlemen's clothes, almost all of them are equally relevant to the upper-class lady's wardrobe so long as you replace 'hat' with 'headscarf', preferably one sporting horses' heads, and 'cavalry twill trousers' with 'tweed skirt'.)

Homo Conservatensis (Upper-class Man)

Tweed cap A comparative youngster, dating from 1960. Replaced 1938 vintage model lost on grouse moor during unfortunate shooting incident. Still being worn in.

Jacket Heavy tweed, Gieves & Hawkes, vintage 1952. Colour bracken/dung. Inadvertently sent for dry-cleaning by valet in 1981. Valet sacked. Elbow patches and leather edging added in 1982 to celebrate the jacket's 30th grouse season.

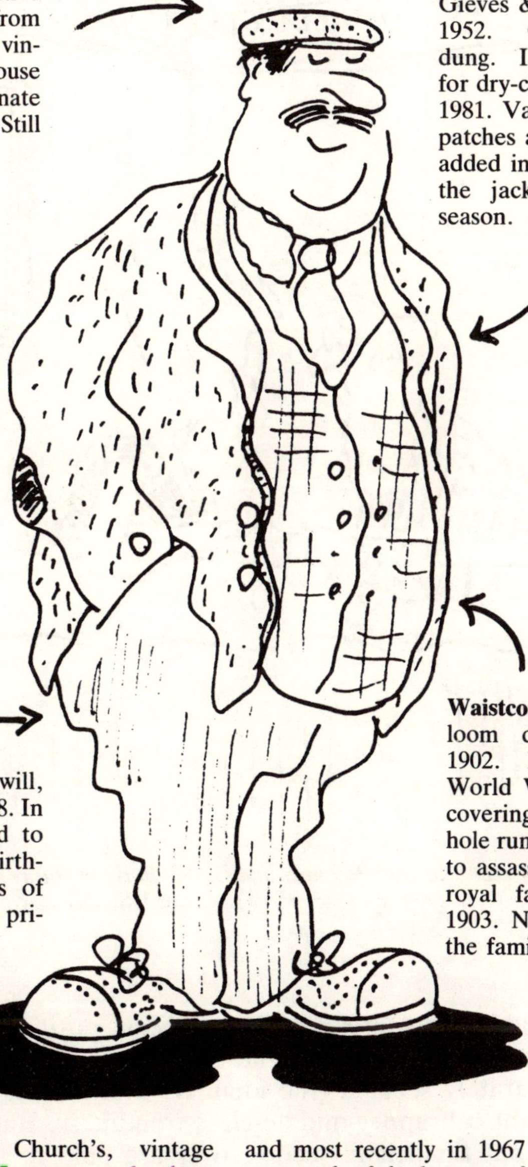

Waistcoat A family heirloom dating from *circa* 1902. Dry-cleaned after World War I but now recovering. Features bullet hole rumoured to be linked to assassination of Serbian royal family on 29 May 1903. Not talked about in the family.

Trousers Cavalry twill, Moss Bros, vintage 1958. In 1983 a party was held to celebrate their 25th birthday. Certain members of Royal Family attended privately.

Shoes Church's, vintage 1948. Lace-up, pale dung colour. Re-heeled in 1952 to celebrate accession of Elizabeth II, again in 1958 to mark the inauguration of Charles as Prince of Wales, and most recently in 1967 as a mark of the last use of steam on Southern Region. Re-soled in 1969 to mark first landing on moon, and again in 1973 when Britain joined the EEC.

UPPER-MIDDLE-CLASS TRENDINESS

'For God's sake don't let Mummy and Daddy find out you're a High Court Judge . . . They'd never let me marry someone who has to work for a living.'

The upper-middle class finds itself in an uneasy position. Stuck between the clearly defined upper class and the solid, run-of-the-mill, middle-middle class, it desperately seeks a true identity. Many of its members find it in what you might call upper-middle-class trendiness. Basically bored out of their minds, but financially secure, they are able to adopt one fad after another, in much the same way that other people change their socks. No fad lasts long, and so the basic character of the upper-middle class constantly shifts over time . . . indeed, the most consistent element of the upper-middle-class make-up is its lack of consistency. A typical pattern of fads might run as follows:

WEEK 1: Role reversal: husband cooks all the meals, changes nappies and collects kids from playgroup, whilst wife keenly attends car maintenance evening classes, smokes a pipe, drinks real ale from straight-sided glasses, and buys the condoms (and incidentally starts to overtake her husband in orgasmic hit-rate).

WEEK 2: Ethnic film craze: taking in at least four products of the Bombay film industry (preferably without sub-titles) during the week followed by an Indian takeaway eaten off additive-free recycled 'Support the Battle Against Acid Rain' paper plates with environmentalist-endorsed bio-degradable plastic cutlery.

WEEK 3: *Nouvelle cuisine*: prepared from high-fibre polyunsaturated free-range soya protein meat analogue and lead-free organically grown vegetables, and served in bijou quantities arranged in exquisite patterns on each plate; severe malnutrition results.

WEEK 4: Sponsoring the education of deprived African children and providing them all with wholemeal, tartrazine-free Filofaxes (with handy condom pocket) manufactured in nuclear-free 'Support Action Against the Destruction of the Ozone Layer' rural communes.

WEEK 5: Family health: everyone cycles between aerobics classes and well-person's clinics dressed in flowing wild cotton peasant dresses or untanned lederhosen after breakfasting on unsweetened orange juice, unsweetened live natural bran-flavoured yoghurt, unsweetened muesli with unpasteurized yak's milk and tannin-free unfermented herbal tea.

WEEK 6: Far East: trips along the Great Wall are planned late into the night over bowls of instant stir-fried shark's fin and spiced duck's webs eaten in Mandarin-style dressing-gowns and Willow Pattern boxer shorts to the accompanying sounds of Linguaphone's 'Teach Yourself Chinese'.

WEEK 7: Anti-ism: everything sexist, racist or ageist is mercilessly banned (Enid Blyton . . . racist and sexist, *Yellow Pages* . . . mainly racist, grandfather clocks . . . ageist, etc.).

WEEK 8: Unbridled polysensual pleasure: chilled champagne washes down beluga caviar in a dewy field beside the Thames near Henley on the morning of the first day of the regatta (it's not *all* bad in the upper-middle class).

And so the upper-middle-class circus goes on. Lots of money and considerable self-confidence are required to keep up the pace, the reward being a totally confusing but deeply fulfilled upper-middle-class lifestyle in which no time or mental energy remains for worrying about one's real identity. Fickle trendiness leaves its mark on upper-middle-class appearance, as the diagram opposite shows.

Homo Trendiensis (Upper-middle-class Person)

Totally natural hairstyle specially created in a Regent Street salon at a cost of £125.

Guy Laroche designer spectacles (Harrods, £350, made in Hong Kong).

Ethnic necklace bought at Sunningdale Ladies Ban Tartrazine in Aid Food for Ethiopia Committee's bring-and-buy sale.

Sponsored bralessness in support of the Wentworth District Free Natural Condoms for Victims of Post-natal Depression in Sudan Action Group.

(Concealed) Natural untreated polyunsaturated cotton open-crutch knickers complete with anti-sex-sterotype condom pocket specially designed to minimize risk of cystitis.

Handmade ethnic leather belt with handy Range Rover key-holder, bought to support the St Edward's Preparatory School Mothers' Action Group Against Acid Rain Pollution Amongst Organic Free-Range Farming Co-operatives in Latvia.

Loose skirt (naturally dyed, peasant-style), handy for coping with unfortunate side-effects of high-fibre and yak-yoghurt diet.

Special designer peasant-style sandals in natural additive-free anti-static buffalo hide picked up for a song (actually £35) at a Weybridge Pony Club white elephant stall.

MIDDLE-MIDDLE-CLASS RESPECTABILITY

The dominant feature of the middle-middle class is without doubt its all-embracing respectability. Without the social standing or self-confidence to stand alongside the trendy upper-middle class, yet desperately wishing to distance itself from the lower-middle, which it sees as a mere step away from the working class, it protects itself with the mantle of respectability. Unfortunately for the middle-middles, gaining such respectability usually involves a high degree of personal sacrifice. Some of the essential accoutrements of this stratum of society are listed below, together with the drawbacks of attainment.

'I've decided we're upper-middle-class, so smarten yourself up a bit today.'

The private road Every middle-middle longs to live in a private road, especially if the houses have names but no numbers. However, the price of such privilege becomes evident in winter, when it becomes impossible to leave the house on the 'unadopted' road without a stout pair of wellington boots or ready access to a Range Rover (unfortunately unaffordable because of the grossly inflated price paid for the house in the private road in the first place).

Private schools, medical care, etc. The cost of these essentials – private education for the offspring and private health care for the whole family – may make it out of the question to get the private road improved, never mind buy the Range Rover.

Riding/ballet/tennis lessons, etc. for the kids As the children go to a private school and mix with others who go for extra-curricular activities in a big way, it is vital for the middle-middle parent to provide the same for his/her offspring. This of course makes it even more difficult to afford the school fees, which in turn puts the Range Rover even further out of reach and thus makes life in the private road even more trying.

Country club membership To the middle-middles membership of a private country club offers unique benefits. It is one place where they can be sure of spending a lot of money in order to mix with people they scarcely know and will probably dislike. Unfortunately this vital social accoutrement does not come cheap, so it makes the riding lessons more difficult to afford, which in turn makes the private school fees even more of a struggle to find, which makes the chances of owning a Range Rover practically non-existent and life in the private road almost intolerable.

Cocktail parties In order to entertain their fellow country-club members, whom they scarcely know and probably dislike, the middle-middles feel obliged to hold extravagant cocktail parties, for which the booze costs about £20 per bottle (after all, they couldn't serve supermarket own-label, could they?). This level of social activity stretches the finances somewhat, rendering membership renewal at the country club quite a problem, the riding lessons almost impossible to afford and the private school fees positively crippling; the likelihood of Range Rover ownership is now roughly on a par with the chances of refuting the Law of Gravity over the breakfast cornflakes.

Gardeners/au pairs/other domestic staff These are a must for any self-respecting middle-middles who wish to keep pace with the people they scarcely know and probably dislike whom they invite to extravagant cocktail parties and whom they met at the country club, the fees for which make it so difficult to find the readies for the riding lessons, the private school fees and the purchase of the Range Rover, without which life in the private road is absolute hell.

And so it goes on. The potholes in the private road get deeper, the chance of owing a Range Rover in which to negotiate the potholes recedes ever further, and thus the middle-middle sinks deeper and deeper into the muddy rut of social respectability. The stress of this sort of life is ingrained in the middle-middle class's appearance, as the diagram* overleaf demonstrates.

*Owing to a slight error at the R&D stage the diagram of the typical middle-middle-class person has been replaced by one of a hydraulic flanging press of the 'Piedboeuf' pattern operating on the Tweddell System. Although this may somewhat diminish the impact of the comments accompanying the diagram the general thrust of the information can still be gathered if the book is held three feet away from the face and the eyes half-closed (and anyway, it's really quite an attractive flanging press as flanging presses go).

Homo Respectabilis (Middle-middle-class Man)

Loss of hair caused by worry about school fees, medical insurance premiums, cost of riding lessons, price of champagne, country club membership fee, etc.

Various impact and fatigue fractures of minor bones caused by driving down private road in unsuitable vehicle (i.e. a car).

Permanently fixed smile caused by trying to maintain the appearance of enjoying oneself whilst paying £1.75 for a half-pint of lager in a country club full of people you scarcely know and don't like, at a cost of £250 per year for membership. Smile also reveals expensive private dental work.

Strained right wrist, caused by constant reaching for wallet to pay for one expensive obligation after another.

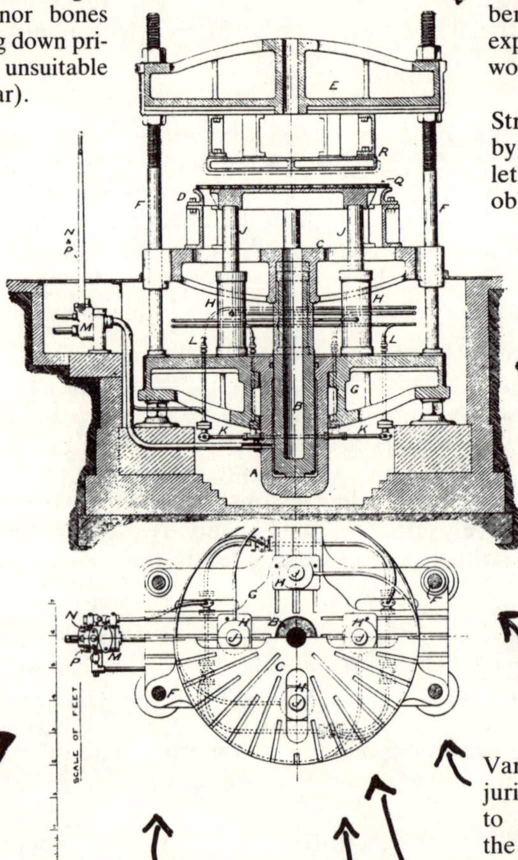

Foot rot caused by excessive wearing of wellington boots to wade through deep flooded potholes in private road.

Housemaid's knee caused by kneeling and praying for things to get better.

Various self-inflicted injuries carried out in order to get some value from the excessively overpriced medical insurance.

In-growing toenails (caused by too much stepping on other people's toes in effort to get on).

Atrophy of sex organs caused by lack of use, the result of worry about money, status, etc.

'As your mother I suppose I ought to be glad there's no risk of your marrying beneath you.'

LOWER-MIDDLE-CLASS COMPROMISE

'This survey here states that more than 85 per cent of middle-class husbands buy their wives dishwashers so they don't have to be chained to the kitchen sink.'

It is inevitable that the middle class should corner the market for compromise, for they are, by definition, a compromise in their own right: neither upper-class nor lower-class, but incorporating elements of both. And there can be no better place to be middle-class than Britain, for Britain itself is one big compromise: not flat, but there again not too hilly; not too warm, but certainly not too cold; part of Europe but still separate . . . and so the compromises go on. In Britain the middle-class compromise is seen at its best amongst the lower-middle class, where it influences, if not controls, almost every aspect of life. For example:

- For the lower-middles the ideal house is a semi-detached: neither a working-class terraced nor a middle-middle detached, but a bit of each rolled into one; terrace on one side, detached on the other – the ideal compromise.
- The ideal place for lower-middles to live is in the suburbs: the lower middles don't want to live right in the town, but there again they would feel slightly uncomfortable living in the country. So they invented the suburb, which is neither whilst being both at the same time, the only place where you can be just round the corner from the shops yet two miles away.
- The perfect lower-middle dog is the mongrel: certainly not the whippet of the working class, nor the labrador of the middle-middles. The mongrel is the ideal compromise: two breeds at the same time without being a member of either.
- Although most of them now live in centrally heated houses, it is amongst the lower-middles that the greatest sentimental desire for an open fire manifests itself. Indeed, such has been the pressure to recapture all the mess and inconvenience of the open fire that there are now imitations powered by both electricity and gas. And the reason is obvious: the open fire is the only form of heating that lets you be both too hot (scorched fronts of legs) and too cold (freezing back and backs of legs) at the same time, the perfect compromise.
- The perfect example of compromise in home furnishings is net curtains: they don't keep the light out, nor do they exactly let it in; they don't really prevent you looking out, but effectively stop you from seeing anything. These are essential lower-middle accessories.
- On the food front, one of the firm favourites of the lower-middles is rice pudding, the perfect compromise between food and something else (although no one has yet managed to establish exactly what).
- The standard lower-middle vacation is two weeks on the Costa del Sol. Foreign, certainly, but at least you can get a decent pint and some fish and chips, and read the *Daily Mirror* every day. The Spanish holiday is the ideal compromise between going abroad and staying at home. And of course when they don't go to Spain, the lower-middles holiday in England, staying in Margate or Worthing, eating paella every night and going flamenco dancing.
- As for religion, the majority of lower-middles will claim to be C of E but never go to church: the perfect religious compromise.
- Many lower-middles are driven by their compromising instincts to vote SLD (Social and Liberal Democrat): in other words neither too far left nor too far right. Otherwise, the 'don't know' category in opinion polls was designed with the lower-middles in mind.
- The ideal lower-middle car is neither too big nor too small, not too new but definitely not too old, not flash but certainly not too run-of-the-mill. A perfect compromise car would be a 2-year-old Ford Cortina 2.0 GL in blue (non-metallic). It is rumoured that at one time Ford were thinking of starting to make 2-year-old Cortina 2.0 GLs just to cater for this enormous market.
- The ideal lower-middle family comprises father, mother, one son and one daughter, with three years between the kids. The working class has as many as, or one more than, it can afford, or as many as nature sends (if not too good at planning). The upper classes have as many as they fancy. But the lower middles have the 'sensible' number, two.

'. . . and to think I turned down a perfectly good offer of marriage from a dustman to marry you.'

- To the typical lower-middle everything is 'nice'. If someone's taste in house decoration is unbelievably appalling, with the sitting room decorated in illuminated fibre-glass cherubs set against a washable vinyl wallpaper of scenes on the Costa del Sol, the average lower-middle would comment, 'That's nice', even if he or she felt like puking. If some typical lower-middles went to a restaurant and were served half-cooked, salmonella-ridden octopus tentacles in a cold custard- and chilli-flavoured sauce and were asked by the waiter if they enjoyed the meal the chances are they'd say, 'Very nice!' prior to throwing up. Such is the all-embracing instinct to compromise.

The compromise is so much a part of lower-middle life that its members often look like compromises, as the diagram shows.

Homo Compromensis (Lower-middle-class Man)

Height: 5′ 10″, a compromise between being a rather short tall person and a fairly tall short person.

The nose: an uneasy compromise between a failed design exercise for the Mersey Tunnel and an olfactory organ.

The moustache: a compromise between filamental facial furniture of epidermal origins and an embarrassing congenital deformity similar to a postage stamp.

The smile: a compromise between benign pleasantry and a facial manifestation of nauseating, toadying, parasitic sycophancy.

The woollen cardigan: a compromise between a sweater and a waistcoat.

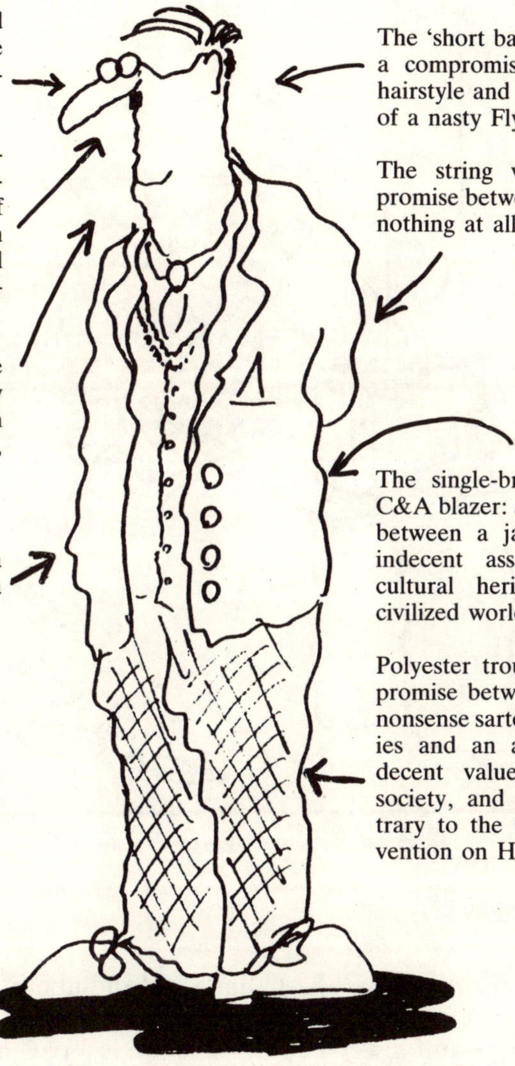

The ‘short back and sides’: a compromise between a hairstyle and the aftermath of a nasty Flymo accident.

The string vest: a compromise between a vest and nothing at all.

The single-breasted green C&A blazer: a compromise between a jacket and an indecent assault on the cultural heritage of the civilized world.

Polyester trousers: a compromise between basic no-nonsense sartorial accessories and an affront to all decent values in human society, and possibly contrary to the Geneva Convention on Human Attire.

LOWER-CLASS ENJOYMENT

'There's a documentary on BBC2 about urban squalor.'

Whereas conservatism is the hallmark of the upper class, fickle trendiness marks the upper-middles, respectability is the millstone round the middle-middles' necks and lower-middle-class life is a pageant of compromise, the outstanding feature of the lower or working class is that, when not working, its members genuinely enjoy themselves. This is a privilege rarely shared by the other classes, and in particular not by the middle class, which is too concerned about what it 'ought' to be doing, or what other people think about what it is doing, to let its hair down and enjoy itself. By contrast, the lower class just has fun! Some examples of *how* it has fun follow.

The annual week in Benidorm Spending a week in the sun, surrounded by exclusively British people of the same class, eating greasy but delicious 'English' fish and chips every night washed down by three good pints of imported English beer, spending the evenings watching shows in English and the morning reading the English papers can actually be quite fun. It's what England itself would be like if only the sun shone. Basically, Benidorm is what Skegness would have been if God had got the design spot-on first time. The average member of the working class feels much more at home in Benidorm than in, say, Weybridge or Sunningdale.

Saturday afternoon TV Spending the afternoon glued to the TV with half a dozen cans of bitter and a packet of fags, watching other people tear around doing appallingly active things like playing football or wrestling, whilst you yourself don't move any muscle which is not directly related to imbibing (thank God for remote control), and then drifting down to the betting shop to collect your winnings and more cans of beer for the evening's sport, can be heaven after a hard week at work.

Sunday morning on the allotment Working-class men have engineered the perfect form of escapism in the shape of the allotment. Under the most laudable guise of all (growing good home-grown vegetables for health and economy) they are able to escape the rigours of household chores and retire to a peaceful haven where they can consume the odd can of beer with other 'gardeners', enjoy a good strong self-rolled fag and read the *News of the World* in peace. Then on the way home they can stop at the corner shop (thank God for Indian corner-shop owners who'll sell you anything, any time of the day, any day of the week) and buy the good home-grown, health-giving and economical vegetables to take home for lunch.

Friday night at the pub Traditionally the working class was paid weekly, in cash, every Friday. There then followed an interesting competition: to see who had the least money left by Saturday morning. The proceedings usually started with a monumental piss-up down at the pub, where eight or ten pints would be happily knocked back without benefit of solid food. The aftermath was scarcely ever remembered as the vital memory cells in the brain were by then dysfunctional, the only certainty being that the following morning most of the money had disappeared, to be replaced by a monumental hangover. Provided this state was achieved it could be acknowledged as having been a 'good' night.

Fishing The lower classes have developed their own form of fishing, known as coarse fishing (the coarseness however applies to the fish, not the fishermen), which is in fact a well-nigh perfect form of sporting activity. Whereas the trout and salmon fishing of the middle and upper classes calls for strenuous efforts even to get to the fishing location and then necessitates continuous exertion of casting and recasting whilst you try to persuade the fish to eat something that bears as much similarity to food as a hangover, coarse fishing is a perfect procedure: you put something the fish really like, such as a maggot or worm, on the end of the line and then go to sleep until the fish decide to give themselves up, indicating their surrender with a polite tug on the line. In other words, coarse fishing is really just an excuse for a quiet snooze by the river listening to the radio, reading *Sporting Life*, or just enjoying a smoke and a cup of tea: pure unadulterated pleasure.

The evening in the pub Whereas the middle classes feel obliged to spend their evenings in 'fashionable' venues such as wine bars, where for about £1 a glass they can drink, amongst total strangers, the same wine they buy from the supermarket for £1.50 a litre and have a thoroughly miserable time, or country clubs where they have the opportunity to consume gin and tonic at £1.80 a time in the company of people they don't really know and probably dislike, the lower classes truly enjoy their nights out at the pub. After all, they have no need to try to 'prove' themselves through their social encounters. Instead, the agenda features beer, darts, beer, dominoes, beer, fruit machine, beer, knees-up by the piano, beer, philosophical discussion about the day's soccer, beer, philosophical discussions about the beer, beer, less than philosophical discussions about the beer, beer and then more beer, and finally down to the Chinese take-away and a couple of cans of beer. Pure, beery bliss!

The characteristic appearance of the lower class, as shown in the diagram opposite, is a direct result of the pursuit of genuine, honest, no-frills enjoyment in life.

'It's not easy to describe you as working-*class!'*

Homo Pleasurensis (Working-class Man)

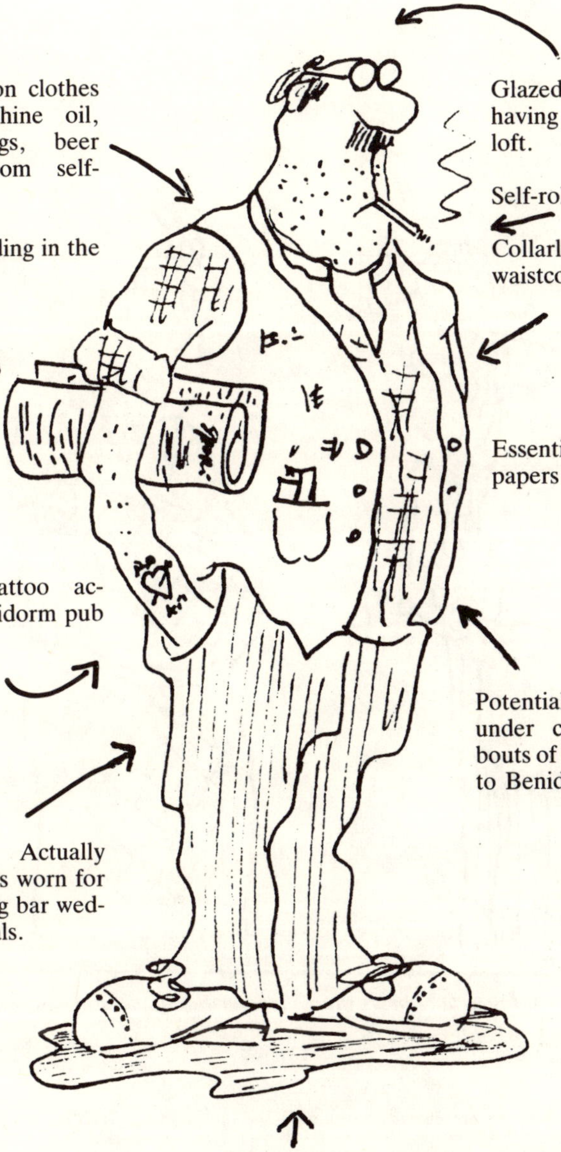

'I think it's going to take more than a leather-bound personal organizer to turn you into a yuppie.'

THE YUPPIE SYNDROME

'I don't think hiding your Filofax is really grounds for divorce.'

The yuppies, a relatively new phenomenon, don't entirely fit into the standard class categories. As young upwardly mobile professionals they aren't upper-class, otherwise they couldn't be upwardly mobile; but there again they can't be lower-class otherwise they wouldn't be professionals. They sit uneasily somewhere amongst the middle-middles and upper-middles, but slightly out on a limb, and they share a common set of problems, which we might call the Yuppie Syndrome*, the main characteristics of which are illustrated overleaf.

* Actually, we could call it the North Peruvian Chicken Rearers' Syndrome, or the Royal Borough of Windsor and Maidenhead Retired Actuaries' Social Club Chorea. I myself fancy calling it a Cornish Pasty as I'm feeling a bit peckish. But to avoid confusion I have referred to it here as the Yuppie Syndrome.

A Absence of clothes reflecting poverty attributable to exorbitant school fees.

B Malformed private parts due mainly to lack of support in boxer shorts and hastily-put-on condoms.

C Typical 'Volvo Neck' caused by attempting to park Volvo 760 Estate in narrow slots on busy high streets.

D Bunion caused by treading on other people's toes in effort to get on after 'Big Bang'.

E Enlarged knee joint caused by driving too fast over unmade residential roads.

F 'Filofax hand', in which the fingers are unable to close round anything thinner than a 'personal organizer' (leather-bound).

G Worry over rise in cost of season ticket causes reversion to use of designer security blanket (cashmere) complete with handy condom pocket.

H Extensive evidence of broken china resulting from adult discussions about where to move to in Docklands.

I Beard grown in effort to blend in at weekends in village in Wilts where cottage has been bought.

J Fear in eyes from worry that road might be adopted and hence used by riff-raff who drive Ford Granadas, drink sparkling wine and eat chicken-in-the-basket.

K Extensive scarring on forehead caused by sharp edge of Golf GTi (16-valve, white) tailgate.

L Hair white from seeing Ford Escort in country club carpark with 'Wayne and Sharon' on windscreen.

M Eyes fixed in sideways glance from constantly checking if neighbour has yet bought Porsche 944 Turbo.

N Deep-rooted Sphinx fixation caused by worry over future of lucrative currency-dealing job in the City, and concern over whether Egypt is still the smart place to go on holiday.

O Lower left arm metamorphosed into cabriole chair leg. Reason totally unknown but blends in well with decoration of town (weekday) flat.

L
M
J
C
A
I
O
B
N
G
I

'You have to admire him . . . Even when he's hit rock-bottom he still manages to preserve some style.'

HOW TO ASSESS YOUR OWN CLASS

Here is a simple, foolproof way of assessing your own social class based on your interpretation of an everyday domestic situation. Examine the picture on page 51, then decide which of the six explanations for what is going on sounds the most plausible. Then interpret your answer as described at the end of the chapter.

Explanation 1 Mrs Davina fforbes-Maitland-Smith (D) shares with her second husband Nigel (E) the revelation that the instant Christmas pudding mix (K) currently being prepared by their transvestite Armenian psychoanalyst, Gerald, who moonlights as a scullery maid (H) to help fund his addiction to cocaine, contains colouring E102 (tartrazine), which possibly explains why the fforbes-Maitland-Smiths' younger son Tarquin (L), provoked by the cat Wittgenstein (M) who insists on rubbing against the boy's leg to the point of feline orgasm, is preparing to knife his sister Rubella (I), aided and abetted by the governess Reginald (A) who, following an only partly successful sex-change operation, has uncontrollable sexual urges towards wicker baskets.

Explanation 2 Mr Wally 'Grouter' Seymour (D), the transsexual shop steward of the Amalgamated Union of Christmas Pudding Mix (K) Operatives, reads the sequestration order delivered by the court bailiff (B) on one of his regular clandestine visits to have kinky sex with the housekeeper. As the Chairperson (H) of the London Borough of Brent's Gay and Lesbian Front Against Spotted Horses (J) Being Given as Christmas Presents mixes food for the flying pickets, members (A and L) of the Popular Front for the Liberation of Wicker Baskets use 'reasonable force' in the shape of knives and scissors to persuade a scab wicker-basket packer (I) to support the unofficial action and join their colleague (G) in doing nothing except sucking a spoon.

Explanation 3 Miss Noni Sidesaddle (D), common-law wife of Mr Julian Sore-crutch (E), mother of their five children (L,I,N,F and G) and secret lover of property developer Monty Fairweather (B), by whom she has had an illegitimate spotted horse (J), confronts her husband with the lost page from his Filofax which reveals that, far from all their money going on a Golf GTi, designer boxer shorts and long weekends at their cottage in the Cotswolds, their dire financial situation results from his clandestine affair with kinky call-girl Ethel 'Steamy' de Lorean (H), who actually works incognito in their house as an apparently innocent middle-aged transvestite kitchen maid. In order to save money and regain financial stability, and to meet the rising school fees for their wayward daughter Nastasia (F), who has rampant incestuous feelings towards Julian, Miss Sidesaddle has decided that in future they will switch to *nouvelle cuisine* and thereby cut out food almost entirely.

Explanation 4 The Hon. Gerald Wymondham-Claverhouse-Cholmondeley-Fiennes (E) shows his wife Caroline (D) his family tree and reveals that, now his younger son (L) and daughter (I) have murdered his elder brother Lord Julian and hidden the body in a wicker basket prior to blaming it on the cat (M), the governess (A) and her lover (J), a Swedish sailor who does very good spotted-horse impressions, there is little to stand in the way of his inheriting the Wymondham-Claverhouse-Cholmondeley-Fiennes fortune, save perhaps for his total inability to remember his own ridiculously long name, a point noted with unnatural interest by the cook, Mrs Spratt (H), who secretly longs to seduce the Hon. Gerald, rob him of his fortune, and elope with her lesbian lover Lucy 'Twinky' Petticoat (B), who visits the house regularly under the cover of being an earthenware jug salesman with an eye for an ugly housemaid.

Explanation 5 Mrs Cecilia Johnston (D) shows her husband Sidney (E) the details of the latest offer from the Frankly-Awful Mint, which practically gives away (at £19.50 per month) a series of individually hand-crafted porcelain Polynesian ear-wax-removing sticks which would complement nicely her nearly complete collection of Victorian life-sized models of children (L, I, N, F and G) and which, taking advantage of the free display cabinet offer, could fill a conspicuous gap on the sitting-room wall behind the last in the series of Dickensian life-sized terracotta servant figurines (H) for which she has just finished paying. Wracked with jealousy, their neighbours (B) plot to purchase on easy terms an electric hedge-trimmer and thereby regain their position of social superiority in Laburnam Avenue.

Explanation 6 The rampantly paedophilic Bishop of Slough, the Very Reverend Ivor Grossewillie (E), surrounded by a number of his recent conquests (L,I,F and N), is finally confronted by a catalogue of his misdeeds by the transvestite Dean of Maidenhead, the Rev. Richard 'Rosie' De Ambrosia (D), whose attempts to infiltrate the Salvation Army and stage a *coup d'état* have been thwarted by an incredibly intelligent wooden toy (J), which speaks through the mouth of an apparently demented tom-cat (M) who has inadvertently super-glued himself to the leg of the boy (L), a non-identical Siamese twin to the patently homicidal, unconvincing Elvis Presley-lookalike Cynthia (A), who has made a feeble attempt to construct an atom bomb inside a wicker basket. The scriptwriter for *EastEnders* (H) looks on, incognito, gleaning ideas for the serial.

B C D E F N K

A L M I J G H

Having decided which explanation sounds most reasonable, interpret your answer as follows:

- explanation 1: your cynical attitude towards the upper-middle class and fascination with transvestite Armenian psychoanalysts indicates that you are of the middle-middle class.
- explanation 2: your contemptuous attitude towards the working class and fascination with transsexuals indicates that you are of the middle-middle class.
- explanation 3: your insecure self-analytical attitude towards the middle-middle class and suspicion of illegitimate spotted horses indicates that you are yourself a member of that class.
- explanation 4: your emotive attitude towards the upper class and fascination with Swedish sailors indicates that you can only be a member of the middle-middle class.
- explanation 5: your demonstrated contempt for the standards of the lower-middle class and your unnatural interest in ear wax indicate that you are a member of the middle-middle class.
- explanation 6: whatever class you belong to (and incidentally, it's the middle-middle class), you're a right kink.

MEASURING YOUR CLASS BY THE F.R.A.P. METHOD

'. . . and the only qualification you've got is "reigning"?'

One of the most reliable (if not most olfactorially satisfying) methods of assessing your own social class is by means of the F.R.A.P. method, or Fart Reaction Amongst Peers method. To distinguish your class you'll need a peer group and a latent fart. If you haven't got or can't get hold of a peer group, then try to borrow one. If you can't borrow one but live near Brighton a pier group will do instead. If you thought a peer group was another name for a collection of peeping Toms, then a group of peeping Toms will do. If you thought a Peeping Tom was a variety of dwarf bush tomato, you're probably reading the wrong book. If you can't summon up a latent fart, delay the test for a day and eat plenty of beans. If this fails any estate agent may be used instead.

Once you have assembled the peer group let the latent fart (or estate agent, if the beans failed you) break loose, hence becoming a patent fart, within clear earshot. Avoid being too close; sitting on one of the peer group's heads during the test might be constituted as bad taste. Assess the peer group's reaction. If one of the following occurs interpret your own class membership accordingly.

- If the majority of your peer group shout, 'Oh my God, I hope the neighbours didn't hear!' as they draw the curtains and start coughing self-consciously to hide any remaining echoes, it would be safe to assume you belong to the lower-middle class.
- If they all look accusingly at each other, you are middle-middle class.
- If the peer group collectively exclaims, 'I say, Nigel, how jolly super! Let's hold a champers-and-farting party . . . Book the Leander, then we could throw the winner into the river . . . How jolly super!!' you might safely assume you belong more to the solid upper-middle class frequented by the jolly rowing Nigels and Henrys.
- If your peer group instantly faints *en masse*, you may gain no real guide as to what social group you belong to, but you sure are a real class farter.
- If the members of your peer group go down on their knees and exclaim, one after the other, 'May I say, Your Grace, that that fart was virtually beyond parallel in the recent history of mankind, and it was an honour to be its witness', it is likely either that you are a member of the upper classes, or that the fart was so bad they'll do anything to flatter you and prevent you doing another.
- If the group totally ignores you, it is likely that you are either very upper-class, where such things pass without mention, or very lower-class, where such things also pass without mention. In all events a null reaction tells you very little . . . except perhaps that you are not the world's most spectacular farter.
- If your peer group breaks up into smaller groups and starts an erudite discussion about E numbers, food additives, the side effects of lead pollution, the destruction of the ozone layer and its effect on the lower digestive system in humans, then you are probably on the intellectual side of the upper-middle or middle-middle class.
- If the peer group spontaneously embarks on a farting competition to outdo you, it is likely that, with such a competitive spirit, it belongs to the middle-middle class. If, however, someone starts a book on who will fart loudest and betting is vigorous, it would seem that there is a certain element of the lower class present.
- If your peer group makes such comments as 'Cor, guv, strike a light . . . that was some raspberry, if you know what I mean, squire!', or 'There's a gesture for the solid farting classes against the oppressive policies of the ruling middle class!' or 'We'll call the lads out!', then you belong to the solid working class.
- If you get comments like 'Have you ever thought of going professional?' then it is safe to say that you belong in the lower-middle class.
- If your peer group drops to the ground breathing deeply and trying to get high on the methane and hydrogen sulphide produced, then you sure have a kinky

lot of peers. If they also strip off their clothes and start flagellating themselves with birch twigs whilst moaning, 'Oh, fart again, please fart again' then I'd consider changing class quickly whichever class you currently belong to.

- If your peer group all open Spanish textbooks and start talking strangely you are in fact a member of an evening class. If it all takes place under water then it's probably a swimming class.
- If your peer group all open Spanish restaurants, God knows what it all means – but steer clear of the paella.
- If all the female members of the group strip off their clothes and start writhing on the floor moaning 'Take me, you masterly farter!', what on earth does it really matter what class you are?
- If the test becomes a regular event and your social life brightens up considerably, you probably belong more to the middle of the middle-middles, for whom normal social life can be a bit drab and any excuse is seized for livening things up a bit.

'God, that was a terrible *nightmare . . . I dreamed our Porsche changed into* last year's *model!'*

HOW MIDDLE-CLASS ARE YOU? – A SIMPLE QUIZ

'We like to have a good social mix at our parties . . . Tonight you're our nominal pleb!'

As you will remember, of the five distinct social classes no less than three are middle classes. Therefore the chances are that any reader taken at random is middle-class (any readers who enjoy being taken at random should contact the author without delay). But just how middle-class are *you*? This series of questions is designed to measure your middle-classness. (Note: we are talking here about *middle*-classness . . . not *upper*-middle-classness with its Henley Regattas and country-house weekends, nor *middle*-middle-classness with its Volvos and coffee mornings, nor lower-middle classness with its privet hedges, D.I.Y. home improvements and evening classes, but *real* middle-classness in its most abstract form.)

'There's some market research bloke out here . . . He wants to know if we're a professional household.'

(1) What is the most significant scientific invention of the twentieth century?
(a) penicillin and other incredible disease-conquering antibiotics which help keep authors fitter to spend more time writing works of wit and erudition for very little money.
(b) the peaceful development of nuclear power for the benefit of all mankind including, I assume, impoverished authors.
(c) fantastically cheap inter-continental air travel, putting the whole world at the disposal of ordinary members of the writing public.

'We've certainly moved to a classy area . . . it says "Hon. Neville Wykeham-Cholmondeley-Fareham-Smythe, Window Repairs and General House Maintenance"!'

(d) the amazing medium of television with its educational, informative and entertainment potential, even though it diverts people from buying and reading books and thereby contributes to keeping authors near the poverty line.
(e) the drip-dry net curtain.

(2) What is the greatest single artistic achievement of the last thousand years?
(a) the *Mona Lisa*.
(b) The ceiling of the Sistine Chapel.
(c) Handel's *Messiah*.
(d) The collected works of William Shakespeare.
(e) *The Reader's Digest Book of Flange Renovation*.

'I just hope that expensive prep school teaches you some table manners!'

(3) What is the most important social duty for anyone living in the twentieth century?
(a) To support his/her family without state aid so they can buy lots and lots of books.
(b) To give back to society (especially authors) more than he/she takes out.
(c) To maintain his/her own health and sanity in order to sustain book-purchasing practice well into old age.
(d) To uphold the law of the land and buy books when instructed to do so by a police officer in uniform.
(e) To keep privet hedges well trimmed.

'It's not that I'm prejudiced against Eton, but . . .'

(4) What is your greatest hope for the future?

(a) That a miracle cure for AIDS and the M25 is found.

(b) That all offensive nuclear weapons and queues on the M25 are abolished.

(c) An end to all famine in the Third World and an increase in the royalties on all paperbacks.

(d) That pollution is kept under control and more paperback books are bought.

(e) That the cost of lawn strimmers is reduced by 10 per cent.

'I thought you said "Come and have a look at my new Porsche" not "Come and have a look at my new porch"!'

(5) If a dangerous criminal were loose in your area what would you do first?
(a) Lock all your windows and doors and phone the police.
(b) Lock away all your valuables, especially paperback books.
(c) Lock away your wife/husband and children.
(d) Get into your car and drive far away, or at least to the nearest bookshop.
(e) Vacuum the carpets and clean the loo in case he breaks in.

(6) What do you think is the secret of a really good picnic in the country?
(a) A crate of vintage champagne, some good female company and a good book.
(b) A crate of beer, some bad female company and a good book.
(c) A crate of women, some good and some bad, and a crate of books, some good and some even better.
(d) A crate of really funny paperback books (Ed.: *That'll scarcely benefit* you, *will it?*)
(e) Clean socks and underwear.

(7) What has been the foremost disaster of the twentieth century?
(a) The two World Wars and resulting loss of potential book-buyers.
(b) The loss of the countryside to industrial and residential development.
(c) The increase in violent crime, which keeps many people indoors when they could be out buying books.
(d) The destruction of the extended family.
(e) The end of *Crossroads*.

(8) Which is the most exciting way to spend a wet Saturday afternoon?
(a) Watching soccer on television with a crate of beer and a funny book.
(b) Trying to burst port-filled condoms by throwing Filofaxes at them from a great height.
(c) Having unbridled sex with a raving-nymphomaniac on a bed of Filofaxes.
(d) Reading the latest book by Keith Ray (Ed.: *You cannot be serious!*)
(e) Putting up a really exciting bookshelf.

(9) What does this this ink-blot look like?

(a) An ink blot.
(b) Two ink-blots (you may have a squint).
(c) The hereditary birthmark of the Dukes of Braunschweig-Helmstedt-Oschersleben.
(d) two official pickets desperately pleading with a scab steelworker not to break a strike.
(e) an ideal design for a fibre-glass ornamental pool-liner.

How to score yourself If you scored less than 3 'e's you are only slightly middle-class. If you scored more than 3 but less than 10 you are middle-class to the core. If you scored betwen 10 and 15 you are both solid middle-class and entirely stupid (or 'muddle-class'). If you scored more than 15 you are a confirmed middle-class liar, but if you say 'e' to everything then you are probably just from the north of England and could be from any class. If you haven't scored at all for weeks, why should you care what class you are? If you're still trying to discover where the ink blot came from you're so stupid it scarcely matters what class you belong to. If you felt the above quiz was slightly biased towards the interests of the author you are, of course, entirely wrong and incontrovertibly middle-class.

'These modern working-class missionaries just don't taste as good as the old upper-class ones used to.'

CLASS AROUND THE WORLD

Class knows no geographical boundaries, and there is very often some correlation between class and personal appearance. With the following hints on identification you will find it possible to go to totally unfamiliar parts of the world yet still be able to pick out an individual's class merely from his dress and mannerisms.

Upper-middle-class. His attempt to reflect the uncompromising self-confidence of the upper class by wearing a cheap lampshade as a hat has been foiled by the action of driving his Volvo Estate down the potholed private road, resulting in a distinct flattening of the lampshade by contact with the car roof

Aspiring middle-middle-class. Having found out that his neighbours have purchased a sit-on lawn-mower, he follows suit and enthusiastically cuts his quarter-acre of grass without even reading the instruction book, hence the long grass clippings caught under his ever-so-naff sunshade.

Vulgar *nouveau riche* lower-middle-class. Having risen above his humble working-class origins and made a small fortune selling garden furniture he now feels a deep-seated psychological urge to flaunt his wealth. In this instance he stuffs half of it into any available body orifice.

Upper-class. This chappie walks around with a strange leather object balanced on his head in the belief that it is some sort of ethnic hat. So self-confident is he that he takes trouble to point out the strange accretion at frequent intervals.

Upper-class again. This chap has been caught exercising his *droit de seigneur*, hence the structural damage to his rather quaint cap caused by contact between his head and the bedroom wall.

Middle-class, endeavouring to imitate the assured self-confidence of the upper classes. This fellow has elected to stick spaghetti all over his face in an attempt to suggest that he couldn't give a fig for what his fellow man thinks.

Lower-middle. In spite of mimicking the upper-middles by means of the Cossack officer-type hat, this chap betrays his true identity (he's a professional snooker-player, i.e. certainly not upper-middle) by carrying the cue around with him.

Middle-middle-class. This fellow has a deep-seated desire to demonstrate his financial security by shaving his entire head, thus indicating that the cost of razors is but nothing to his bank account. His lack of upper- or upper-middle self-confidence stops him going the whole hog, hence the strange remnant at the front.

Any man who decides to wear the top of a boudoir stool on his head and then look away from everyone, hence drawing attention to the unconventional headgear, is almost certainly upper-middle. He is suggesting, even advocating, that boudoir stools are the latest thing in hats.

Middle-middle-class. This man would like to dress in smart, fashionable clothes, but has to wear old velvet curtains instead: a sad case of attempting to ape the upper-middles but, lacking the income, finding the school fees just a little too much.

Upper-middle-class. A clear case of a comfortable upper-middle who has nothing better to do than muse over the fundamental conflict between the auto-regressive id-motivated Oedipus complex and the desire to dress as a transsexual Jesuit priest.

Aspiring lower-middles. In the desperate fight to upgrade their personal means of conveyance from a Sierra L to a Sierra GL these two are willing to forgo clothes and resort to body paint instead. Not the sort of thing that would be allowed in Tunbridge Wells.

Upper-class. Having gone bald he prefers to wear an old mop on his head rather than a wig, even though the mop handle remains visible. Typical upper-class self-confidence. Also a typical upper-class twit.

Face clearly wracked with self-doubt, here is a good example of recently elevated lower-middle class. Should you pout in public? Is a tight, frizzy perm a good idea? Is an old beach towel the right dress for Henley? . . . Clearly all these questions are at the forefront of his mind.

Difficult to place, this one. A man who opts to wear part of a weather station inverted on his head could be a solid middle-class professional (a weather forecaster, perhaps), or upper-class uninhibited, or quite simply a congenital wally from any stratum of society.

CLASS AND SMELL

You do not need a highly developed sense of smell to know that each class has its own unique 'smellprint', which allows each to identify other members of the same even across a crowded room.

The main olfactory characteristics of each stratum of society are as follows:

The upper class A synonym for upper-class is high-class, and the real significance of the word 'high' lies in its olfactory context. The essential components of the upper-class smell are:

- a hint of wet labrador crossed with freshly caught salmon
- a nuance of damp tweed nurtured in equine sweat
- a suggestion of unventilated stable with just a soupçon of gun oil, Earl Grey tea and kedgeree
- a tantalizing aroma of wellington boot crossed with damp marquee, expensive cigars and old, cracked leather.

This smell does not vary; it can't, because the clothes are generally not changed or cleaned. A good tweed jacket, like a pair of hand-made brogues, is not worn in until it is a good ten years old, and does not reach its prime for a further quarter of a century; dry-cleaning would upset its complex bio-system, itself intensified by the dark-patterned handkerchief (changed every August whether dirty or not). The smell simply gets stronger in warm weather, as the jacket loosens up, and weaker in cool weather, as the jacket gets stiffer again. The great thing about the upper class is that, like the working class, it doesn't get hung up on smell. Also, traditionally, even if upper-class people *did* smell they could do little about it, as their plumbing was so antiquated and eccentric. Moreover, body odours remind them of childhood, the nursery and Nanny. So it's hardly surprising that the upper class has remained a class apart . . . no one with a sensitive nose would go near them!

The upper-middle class Descending to the upper-middles, we find that the smell has changed radically. For a start, we have hit the bidet stratum, and many of the traditionally upper-class body smells have been washed away rather than flaunted (like those of the uppers) or concealed (like those of the middle-middles). As a result, the upper-middles are virtually smell-free, often possessing just a faint hint of carbolic. This social stratum changes its clothes frequently, and so what smells remain are clear and distinct; at one moment, therefore, we'll get a faint hint of riding stable, the next a whiff of prep-school cloakroom, next a faint odour of Range Rover giving way in turn to gin-and-tonic crossed with Barbour. The upper-middles have a smell for every occasion and wear them with carefully designed pride.

The middle-middles At the middle-middle level strong odours are again apparent, fuelled by an obsessive desire to conceal all smells which might have a vaguely human origin. The middle-middles have a deodorant for every area and orifice of

RAY
MEN'S TOILETRIES
NEW
ARISTO
WET GUNDOG
DAMP TWEED
EAU DE STABLE

the body: under-arm, crutch, vagina, earlobe, foot, mouth . . . given time, marketing whizz-kids could no doubt find a way of selling the middle-middles deodorants for the nostrils, navel, eyeballs and endocrine system.

The exception to all this is that substratum of middle-middles who have returned to Mother Earth and have deliberately cultivated an aroma of hessian sacks, old sandals and wholemeal flour – often accompanied by a hint of incense redolent of their origins as children of the swinging 'sixties.

The lower-middles The lower-middles are generally too shy and unassertive to smell of anything too distinctive. The men, whilst not wishing to smell of sweat, are equally wary of the risk of being called a poof if they smell of perfume, and the women lack the money to purchase the fragrance of true sophistication. As a result they usually smell of nothing apart from cooking, gloss paint, Milton fluid, bleach, the 5.25 from Paddington and the thousand-and-one other odours picked up by a normal person on a normal day. Such normality is rigorously exchanged on social occasions for a barrage of Brut, hair lacquer and cheap, flowery perfume, to be gradually displaced by the insistent whiff of the alcohol they consume at such times.

The working class The working class shares a great deal, from an olfactory point of view, with the upper class. Basically its members have an honest approach to smell. If they work in a foundry they get sweaty and therefore smell of sweat; to replace the lost body fluid they drink beer and smell of beer; when they've had too much beer they throw up and start to smell of . . . and so it goes on. Such honesty is shared only by those at the opposite end of the social scale.

If you wish to elevate the class to which your fellow man perceives that you belong, here is a simple technique for achieving it. Simply take a new dog lead, soak it overnight in gun-oil and leave it outside in damp grass wrapped in a well-used fishing net and covered in a 6-inch layer of stable sweepings. Then pour half a bottle of gin over it and dry it out in a stack of Havana cigars. Wear this day and night next to the skin, without bathing, for two months. Finally, let an ageing golden retriever chew it for a couple of hours. The lead will then be ready for use; if ever you wish to give an impression of high social standing simply wear the lead round your neck under your clothes. As your bodily warmth permeates the lead the mélange of odours will be released and your perceived social standing will climb accordingly.

CLASS AND SEX

'Oh, by the way, I've told my Dad you're a barrister.'

Class and sex are closely linked. The various social classes put different levels of effort into sexual relationships and have varying expectations from them. What follows is a general guide to sexual attitudes and practices up and down the social spectrum. But beware – there are always variants. Not all upper-middle-class people are upper-middle-class in their sexual habits; a duke may behave like a navvy in bed, whilst a stevedore may treat his partner like a lady.

The upper class To the upper class sex has two quite distinct functions. First there is a duty to continue the ancestral line, and secondly there is the satisfaction of animal lust. Ideally these two functions should be fulfilled with different partners. Breeding is shut-your-eyes-and-think-of-England stuff, in which pleasure is scarcely thought about and even more rarely experienced; often the 'brood mare' is too tall for lips and sexual organs to be brought into contact at the same time, and the aristocratic noses may well be too long for satisfactory kissing unless the heads are at right angles to each other, in which position sex – at any rate sex with that same partner – becomes impossible anyway. Many upper-class types derive more pleasure in bed from the warmth of a loyal red setter than they do from copulation. Foreplay may be a gin and tonic and a good cigar over a game of billiards and a discussion about pheasant hatching rates, whilst the afterglow usually consists of another, even bigger, g-and-t over a second frame. By contrast the animal lust can be satisfied with a partner of any class, sex, size and species . . . and often is.

The upper-middle class The main feature of upper-middle-class sex (when it actually takes place at all, that is . . . many of this sort are so busy trying to be successful in careers they have no time for it) is that it *must* appear to be totally liberated. Bodies are natural and should be seen, so upper-middle-class parents walk around the house naked to demonstrate to their children that there is nothing dirty about nudity, and have baths without locking the door. The fact that many of them when naked look like wrinkled, geriatric sacks of mouldy potatoes with hairy armpits, hairy chests and hairy legs (*both* parents: after all, it's natural to have hair) grossly embarrasses the children, who would actually rather look at TV. Indeed, it's a wonder the youngsters aren't put off sex for life. Essential equipment includes boxer shorts with condom pockets, unashamedly phallic vibrators, and *Thompson's Dictionary of Orgasms*; this doesn't exist, but if it did it would be a sure-fire bestseller amongst the upper-middles who think multiple orgasms are compulsory, the missionary position is a sign of failure, rubber is fun, if Mars bars help that's fine, and that sex is *meant* to be noisy, with squeaking beds, writhing and moaning . . . and if the children overhear that's fine too, as it's all perfectly natural wholemeal, free-range, additive-free copulation.

The middle-middle class The middle-middles are the cautiously adventurous but incredibly insecure ones. Being obsessively conscious of the prudish attitude of the lower-middles, with whom they dread being confused, they go out of their way to work out how far they should go with sexual experimentation. They buy most of the sex manuals and often fall asleep while struggling with the intricate anatomical details. They consume the most pre-coital alcohol in an attempt to forget their insecurity. They have had it drummed into them that foreplay is important, and that orgasms come in different types and sizes, and sometimes don't even happen at all. They keep mental records of sexual frequency, orgasmic hit-rate, time to orgasm, ratio of foreplay to real action, and inter-copulatory down-time, because their fundamental insecurity makes them feel obliged to be totally normal (anything less than normal sexual frequency might indicate latent homosexuality). Impotence is like a death sentence, as it ruins all the sexual ratios. It is vital to the middle-middles that they conform to the sexual norms outlined in the Kinsey reports. If they're dropping behind the norm they feel obliged to catch up even if they're on the point of exhaustion and not in the mood . . . and then they force themselves to moan, use two different positions and try it again in the shower just to appear totally normal.

The lower-middle class The lower-middle class is by far the most prudish of the classes in bed. Sex is fine so long as it's done with the lights off, both partners are fully clothed, the bed doesn't squeak, the children can't hear, the door is locked, the next day is not a working one, the cat's out, all the bills have been paid, and there's not a vowel in the month. Sex is never ever contemplated during the woman's period, during daylight, or in strange beds, and is always carried out on the same night of the week at the same time (the 'early night') and in the same position . . . strictly missionary. Ideally sex would be carried out in complete silence with neither partner moving, or even touching, and any post-coital feelings of goodwill transmitted by typed memorandum with two carbons. This pre-planned, mechanical, sterile activity is characterized by a euphemistic 'nudge-nudge, wink-wink, say-no-more, squire' type of language of its own. Indeed, it's a miracle the lower-middles ever manage to reproduce at all.

The working class The working class has a totally different attitude to sex. The man sees it as his right, to be exercised after every visit to the pub (have a drink, have a walk, have a bag of chips, have a woman), whilst the wife, although occasionally enjoying it, or at least the slap-and-tickle preamble, more often just lies back and thinks of bingo. Often, because of cramped housing and the multiplicity of kids, sex has to be carried out in the dark, as does undressing. In fact many working-class couples have never seen each other naked, which can be a great advantage. In the dark she can look like Page 3 (flat, and by the evening crumpled) whilst he could pass for Paul Newman, albeit slightly rearranged. Impotence is rarely a problem; erections come and go regularly like working shifts, and when the shift starts the task is completed according to standard working practices. If strikes do occur, they are unfortunate but are blamed on somebody else (the wife, the dog, the kids, the government, the beer, etc.).

35 Wych Elm Rd,
Hornchurch,
Essex.
27th May 1991.

Gama International Ltd.

Reference charact

'Mummy, you must meet Derek . . . He's not good-looking or rich or anything, but he is *a chartered accountant!'*

'A 300-foot-high pile of stone! That's a bloody stupid sort of status symbol!'

FAMOUS CLASS-RELATED EVENTS IN HISTORY

From the very earliest days when Adam and Eve were expelled from the Garden of Eden and forced to become the first members of the suburban middle-class, riddled with middle-class hang-ups about fig leaves, serpents and apples, history has been riddled with class-related struggles and the clash of one set of class values with another. Described below are some of the more significant of the events which have helped shape society as we know it today.

The Domesday Book In 1086 William the Conqueror, who was by nature an exceptionally well-organized person and one of the first yuppies in history (his upward mobility took him from Normandy, with its appalling Golden Delicious, to England, with its decent Cox's Orange Pippins – definitely a move up in my opinion), mislaid his Filofax and thereby lost all record of what his new kingdom contained. Finding the strain almost unbearable, he commissioned a major rewrite of the crucial missing pages and inserted them into his new Filofax in the telephone-number section (largely because he couldn't think of anything else to put there, the invention of the telephone still being a good 800 years away). However, the shock of being without his Filofax for even a few months proved too great for William, and in the following year he died, a victim of that dreaded disease MPOS (Missing Personal Organizer Syndrome).

The painting of the Sistine Chapel In 1507 Mike Angelo, as he was then known, was a run-of-the-mill but quite intelligent painter and decorator specializing in churches, chapels, municipal baths and government offices. It was in the autumn of that year, whilst doing up the gents' loos in Whitehall Palace, that he picked up an old copy of the *Burke's Classification of Occupations* and discovered, to his dismay, that painters and decorators were rated as Class IIIM (skilled manual) alongside plumbers, electricians (of which there were none) and TV repair men (of which there weren't any either). Being an ambitious sort of chap and wishing to marry above his station (for money, as he didn't really enjoy slapping on whitewash), he decided to seize every opportunity whilst painting and decorating (Class IIIM) to demonstrate his skills as an artist (Class II) and thereby improve his station in life. He also changed his name to Michelangelo Buonarroti, which he thought sounded more classy, although his mates in the painting and decorating trade thought it sounded a bit effeminate. In 1508 his big opportunity arose when the Pope, who'd had a spot of pebble-dash on the Vatican repaired by Angelo's firm, noticed that the interior of his chapel was looking decidedly grubby and asked him to whitewash it. Michelangelo realized that if, instead of whitewashing the ceiling, he executed

'His Grace, the Duke, has a headache, and he's asked that you, as his valet, should deputize for him.'

instead a monumental masterpiece based on a series of scenes from the Creation to the Drunkenness of Noah, featuring a great many nude youths (confirming his workmates' worst fears), prophets and sybils, the Pope might take more notice. What is not well known is that once the ceiling was finished the Pope sacked him, because he really couldn't abide monumental masterpieces, prophets and sybils, but on the other hand he loved, and indeed had a strange fetish about, whitewash.

The building of the Great Wall of China The Great Wall actually started life as the world's longest and most impressive privet hedge. In 222 BC the Emperor Qin Shi Huang married an exceptionally middle-class wife (an event not generally recorded in official textbooks because of the subsequent embarrassment of employing 256,000 men to keep the hedge trimmed) who insisted that he planted the hedge so that potential invaders from the north could not see into anyone's living room. A couple of years later the Emperor's wife took a fancy to a set of terracotta gnomes

'I must confess there are days when I regret abdicating.'

(well, actually, 2,729,667 of them) and wanted to display them at intervals along the hedge, but of course the hedge couldn't take the weight, so a wall had to be built instead. Several centuries later the embarrassment of having the greatest wall in the world topped by 2,729,666 gnomes (one was dropped during construction, for which 3,889,220 workers were slaughtered as punishment . . . it was tough in those days) proved too great and the gnomes were removed and buried. The terracotta army at Xian is in fact one of the burial places, but again the embarrassment of showing an army of garden gnomes, however ancient, was too great for the Chinese and they were replaced by model soldiers instead.

Hannibal's journey across the Alps Hannibal's real reason for crossing the Alps was so that he could feel socially superior. In Carthage in 218 BC generals were two-a-penny and counted for nothing socially, whereas in Italy, owing to a total lack of indigenous elephant trainers, Hannibal stood a chance within his new occupation of marrying well and buying himself out of the army. This he failed to do in the end, largely because the elephants scared the hell out of all eligible young ladies.

Dissolution of the monasteries This episode is the best-documented effort in the sixteenth century to break up a closed-shop agreement between the National Union of Monastery Workers and the employers' representative, the Pope. Subsequently the monasteries accepted workers from a variety of affiliations including the Society of Gregorian Chant Operatives, the Association of Cloister Workers, the National Union of Habit-wearers and Allied Trades and the Transport and General Celibate Workers' Union. This soon became too much for the employers' side and under impossible pressure to settle unrealistic wage claims in total silence and celibacy, the monasteries closed one by one.

The siege of Troy The underhand tactics by the Trojan management to break through the Greek picket line outside the city and bring in scab kebab-house workers inside a wooden horse have gone down in the history of the trade union movement as the greatest class struggle since the Tolpuddle Martyrs (I know this sounds anachronistic, but 'the greatest struggle since the Tolpuddle Martyrs' sounds better than 'the greatest struggle *before* the Tolpuddle Martyrs').

Noah's Ark This was the inevitable and by now well-known result of a sit-in at a closed-down shipyard where the workers continued to build unwanted arks (most of the ark work having been taken by the as-then-undiscovered Far Eastern yards . . . clever, those Japanese, even when you don't yet know they exist). Fortunately for 'Red' Noah, the workers' co-operative leader, the rains came and the market for arks experienced an upturn. Unfortunately the rains also washed the shipyard away.

Paul Revere's ride Revere's desperate ride from Boston to Lexington was not to warn the revolutionary leaders of their imminent arrest by the British, but to obtain a supply of clean boxer shorts as those available in the Boston area lacked the handy condom pocket so valued by eighteenth-century American patriots.

The building of the Great Pyramids Back in the days of ancient Egypt it was not possible to demonstrate your social superiority over your neighbour by possessing a Ford Sierra 2.0 GL in cases where he has to make do with a 2.0 L or, worse still, a 1.6. Instead of cars, sit-on lawn-mowers, video cameras and boats, the Egyptians had to make do with such status symbols as sphinxes and pyramids. The more important you were, the bigger the pyramid you were given. Of course, as with cars today, many pyramids were actually company pyramids; these were a common perk, but pretty useless ones really as you couldn't do much with your pyramid except die inside it. If you were something really big in Cairo you could have an exceptionally large pyramid. The Great Pyramids were the Ford Scorpio 2.8 Ghias of their day.

The discovery of gravity A successful attempt by an orchard worker (Class IIIM, manual skilled) to leap two classes and become a scientist (Class I).

'It's not that Henry's an accountant . . . it's just that your mother and me don't want you to marry beneath you.'

NAMES AND CLASS

Christian names, or rather forenames, are a telling reflection of a person's class, actual or aspired-to. The link has been built up over many generations and is now a robust part of the class structure. Although there is some blurring of the edges, the following observations generally apply.

The working class Like the very top echelons of society, this class is quite adventurous with names; names flit in and out of favour from year to year, or even week to week as one TV soap opera finishes and a new one begins, or a new Mills & Boon novel appears. Amongst the real favourites are the so-called Ford-Escort-windscreen names, the sort you see in carefully sexed pairs in large self-adhesive letters on the inside of the car windscreen. Popular examples include:

Wayne	Tracey	Craig	Kelly	Michelle
Sharon	Lee	Damien	Darren	Lorraine
Jason	Kerry	Kylie	Dean	Donna

Nothing better complements the appearance of the 5-year-old Ford Escort, with its flaired arches (but not yet the wide wheels to go with them), spoilers and tinted glass, than a set of 'Wayne & Tracey' stickers.The real acceptance criterion is whether the name sounds right when prefixed by 'Our . . .' (pronounced 'Ow-er' not 'R'); hence 'Our Damien', 'Our Lorraine' and 'Our Sharon' sound just right, whereas 'Our Nigel', 'Our Quentin' and 'Our Henry' do not. Sometimes the genre is taken one step further by being hyphenated, hence the Tracey-Diane, Kerry-Louise and Michelle-Jane which self-consciously bridge the gap between adventurous working-class names and safe lower-middle-class ones. This class-bridging occurs only between neighbouring classes, so we don't for example get Wayne-Nigel, Kelly-Caroline and Damien-Bamber. Another feature of these names is that you can often predict the age of their owners by remembering when a character with the same appellation was popular on TV; hence many Jasons were born when Jason King was still popular on TV. Indeed, so many of these names derive from television that there is a risk that novel new names, hybrids of soap-opera heroes and washing-up liquids, may be unintentionally created.

The upper class None of the above-mentioned names would be suitable for the upper class, which goes instead for the highly traditional Charles, Henry, William, Caroline, etc. These names are chosen because new additions to the family *always* have to be called Charles, Henry, etc. The fact that they sound ludicrous when applied to a tiny baby is hardly relevant, because in the real upper-class family a child is scarcely ever called by its forename until it is about 18. The child's main adult contact is with the nanny, who calls the child 'Master Charles' or 'the young

Master', which sound OK, whilst at school all the boys call each other by their surname even if they are brothers. Indeed, many upper-class children leave their public school scarcely remembering their own first names because it is so unfamiliar. The total unsuitability of the Ford Escort names for the upper class is due to a number of factors:

- the individual concerned may be the heir to a title or could be knighted in adulthood. Whereas 'Sir Charles' sounds great when announced by a toast-master, 'Sir Wayne and Lady Tracey' leaves something to be desired.
- they may have parks, almshouses or awards named after them, and whilst the 'Charles Henry Leigh-Comberbach Memorial Hospital' sounds dignified, some of the dignity evaporates when you substitute Darren or Jason.
- they don't drive Ford Escorts or watch soap operas, or if they do they would never admit to it. (And if they did they could afford the wide alloy wheels to go with the flared arches.)
- the name must sound right when shouted at 2 a.m. across the court of a Cambridge college during May Week by a less-than-sober undergraduate. 'Hey, Nige, old chap, throw us down a magnum of champers!' may be OK, but 'Hey, Wayne' sounds more like a Constable painting than a friendly request.

At the extremes of the upper classes, and the outer reaches of the professional upper-middles, where self-assurance reigns supreme, names may be as adventurous as you wish; if the parents wish to call their son Bamber, Marmaduke, Christmas, Norrington, Pashley, Architrave, Viscera or Composta, then they do just that. Why should *they* care about other people's reactions?

The middle class In between the extremes of upper and working class lies the wide spectrum of middle-class names. One group of names worthy of note is the so-called Range Rover names: the ones that run smoothly off the tongue when called out across the car park of an expensive prep school from the window of a Range Rover and are characteristic of the upper end of the middle-middle and lower half of the upper-middle. Among favourites are Rupert, Nigel, Oliver, Jennifer, Victoria and Alexandra. The important criterion is that they sound just right in greetings like:

> 'Rupert, darling, don't forget the *au pair* is collecting you tonight.'
> 'Nigel, darling, isn't that *nice*? Victoria's invited you to tea and a swim at her house after your riding lesson!'
> 'Do hurry, Alexandra, dear. Mummy'll be late for her hair-do, and it's Henley tomorrow!'
> 'We've finally decided on Charterhouse for little Oliver.'

Waynes don't have *au pairs*, Traceys by and large don't have friends with swimming pools, Craig's parents don't go to Henley and few Darrens are educated at Charterhouse. The middle classes are the ones who worry most about names. They're the ones who buy those little books of Christian names and go through with a yellow highlighter picking out all those that are socially acceptable; they'll also look at the *Times* birth column (probably the only time they'll actually read *The Times*) to choose a name that the 'top people' might choose. The upper class doesn't have the luxury of such a choice, whilst the working classes don't need to consult anything other than the *TV Times*.

'I hope you're not sharing your cell with any common types!'

'Our Wayne can't decide between the music scholarship to Radley and the place at Eton.'

CLASS STRUGGLE

'Typical capitalist ploy . . . trying to buy us off with enormous pay increases and shorter hours just because things are going well!'

Class struggle, the struggle of the under-class against the class it believes to be the oppressor, is much older than many people realize. It dates from long before the Tolpuddle Martyrs; indeed it probably started when some poor downtrodden caveman, feeling he had been denied his fair suck at the rancid putrefying pig's carcase on offer for lunch, ripped out his master's lower intestine and used it to throttle him whilst uttering that well-known battle-cry 'Arrrrrrrgggghhhhhhhhhhh, that'll teach you, you nauseating mass of bovine by-product!' Class struggle was going strong in the seventeenth century when Charles II was restored to the throne, as the contemporary engraving shown here illustrates.

1
7
6
4
8
2
9
3
10
5
KING CHARLES II.
triumphal Entry into the City of London at his Restoration

1 Disguised as a statue of Justice a shop steward of the Union of Builders of Appallingly Vulgar Ceremonial Arches waits to drop a 15-tome petition on the King's carriage.

2 Owing to appallingly low wages the standard bearers are obliged to wear old flags as clothes.

3 Two transsexual theatrical horse operatives pretend to be the King's horse prior to kidnapping him and claiming a £1,000,000 ransom to help support the Westminster Campaign Against AIDS Tests on Royal Animal Impersonators.

4 Four members of the Union of Timber-framed Prefab Hovel-builders attempt to build a timber-framed hovel over the King's head prior to blowing it up in protest at mortgage tax relief being limited to the first 1*s* 6*d* of each loan on prefab timber dwellings.

5 The royal procession follows a tortuous route owing to the absence of white lines following an unofficial strike by local authority white-line artists.

6 All middle-class suburban gardens have been removed for the procession, resulting in a total absence of garden gnomes.

7 Almost no members of the public watch the procession because all the yuppie residents are away for the weekend at their cottages in Wiltshire.

8 A typical middle-class family attempts to protest against a 2-guinea tax on double-page yearly planner pages for leather-bound Filofax personal planners and the shortage of private nursery-school places.

9 A group of upper-middle-class loyalists proudly displaying on top of their heads the latest in designer tea-cosies.

10 Charles's friend Nigel attempts to lobby the King on behalf of the London Borough of Brent's Gay and Lesbian Committee for Free Condoms and Boxer Shorts for People at the Back of Regal Processions.

'Well, that's nothing*! My father's chauffeur's footman's gardener's chauffeur has a chauffeur-driven Bentley,* so there*!'*

HOW TO CREATE AN ILLUSION OF CLASS WITH YOUR CHILDREN'S HELP

If you feel you lack class and wish to create an illusion of being from a higher social stratum than you really are, there are few better allies you can have than your own children. With a little bit of careful coaching, and a few strategically used phrases, children can create an aura around their parents which will impress even the most socially presumptuous. The phrases listed below are most powerfully used outside the school gates when your little allies are being dropped off or collected, and must be used within earshot of the largest possible number of other parents. A note of caution, however: the phrases are designed simply to create an illusion of grandeur, and it is therefore crucial that other parents never see through the pretence. This may in practice require you to be a social leper, but you can't have everything. Get your kids to learn the following phrases for use on demand:

- 'Mummy, can I lend Victoria one of my ponies? She's only got one and it's gone lame.' This should be countered by something like 'But darling, you *know* they're all at Newmarket at the moment at the stud.'
- 'Mummy, what's a "kitchen"? Do *we* have one?' The natural response to this is 'I *think* so, darling. Isn't that the place where Cook and her helpers prepare the meals?'
- 'Daddy, please, oh please, can Daniel come and play in our swimming pool? The *indoor* one, I mean, of course.' This is best countered by something like 'Oh dear, you know the indoor pool is out of action while the new heating system is being installed. It'll be so much nicer for you and your friends to play in when it's all done.'
- 'Daddy, I swapped that House of Lords notepaper. Can you get me some more when you next go?' A good response to this is 'But I only go for the State Opening . . . and that's a *long* time off.'
- 'Mummy, Alexandra's parents have such a funny garden – it's only about two acres. And did you know? They do all the gardening themselves!'
- 'Daddy, why do some parents do their own gardening? Do they *like* getting dirty?'
- 'Daddy, I thought you said *everyone* has their own vineyard.'

- 'Daddy, can we hire Concorde again for my birthday?'
- 'Mummy, Daddy, do we *have* to go on the *QEII* this year? I'll miss the biology field trip!'
- 'Daddy, why don't we use our title?' This is best countered by 'I never know which one to use, dear.'
- 'Mummy, Simon's parents live in a house that's actually joined to someone else's. Isn't that fun?'
- (When riding in some other parent's car) 'Where's the telephone? And don't you have a cocktail cabinet and TV?'
- (When at a friend's house) 'You mean your mummy actually cooks the food herself?'
- (At friend's house, asked naively of the parents) 'Where does the chauffeur live? And where are all the other servants?'
- (To friend) 'It seems so strange your daddy being plain "Mr" Jones.'
- (At a friend's house on Saturday afternoon when *Grandstand* is on) 'Can I see whether one of my daddy's horses is racing at Doncaster?'
- 'Mummy, Alex's parents have only got one house. Where do they go at weekends?' A good reply is 'I expect they go abroad.'
- 'Daddy, there's a new boy in our class, and his daddy actually goes out to work every day!'

To reinforce the illusion created by such phrases, thorough preparation is necessary. First, take care to arrive at school in the right sort of vehicle. Expensive cars may be hired (but remember to remove any Avis or Hertz stickers, and make sure the car is dirty) but it is always acceptable to use a Land Rover, and they are relatively cheap; secondhand and slightly battered is fine. A little time spent under a sunlamp will create the impression of a life of leisure and travel to warmer climes. And remember always to be seen in casual, not excessively smart, clothes when dropping the kids in the morning, even if this necessitates a hasty change into your working suit round the corner. Casual clothes mean there is no need for you to earn a living, and not needing to earn a living spells class.

'What does "degenerate ruling class" mean, Mummy?'

'I'm always delighted to see a working-class lad get on in this company, Jones . . . It's a shame you're not going to be the one.'

A FINAL WORD

Having read this book the reader may legitimately enquire whether class really matters; after all, class doesn't guarantee that you'll live longer, be fitter, be better-looking or have a more exciting sex life, or even be more comfortable and better-off. After all, many aristocrats live from hand to mouth trying to keep their crumbling stately homes in order whilst many working-class people live in comparative luxury.

So *does* class matter? Well, if you don't mind crawling around in the lower strata of the festering dungheap of society whilst the Hooray Henries of this world metaphorically puke all over you with contemptuous disregard, then you're welcome to it . . . Personally, I'll struggle to clamber as far up the dungheap as possible – so there!

'He was such an appalling snob!'